9781328 11287

To Celebrate

_____

_____

Date

_____

THANK YOU FOR COMING.

Let's celebrate!

Guest Name

_____

Wishes & Messages

_____

_____

_____

_____

_____

_____

_____

✉ Email/Phone

Guest Name

_____

Wishes & Messages

_____

_____

_____

_____

_____

_____

Email/Phone

Guest Name

_____

Wishes & Messages

_____

_____

_____

_____

_____

_____

EMAIL/PHONE

Guest Name

_____

Wishes & Messages

_____

_____

_____

_____

_____

_____

_____

EMAIL/PHONE

Guest Name

_____

Wishes & Messages

_____

_____

_____

_____

_____

_____

_____

✉ Email/Phone

Guest Name

_____

Wishes & Messages

_____

_____

_____

_____

_____

_____

Email/Phone

Guest Name

Wishes & Messages

Email/Phone

Guest Name

_____

Wishes & Messages

_____

_____

_____

_____

_____

_____

Email/Phone

Guest Name

_____

Wishes & Messages

_____

_____

_____

_____

_____

_____

_____

Email/Phone

Guest Name

_____

Wishes & Messages

_____

_____

_____

_____

_____

_____

_____

Email/Phone

Guest Name

_____

Wishes & Messages

_____

_____

_____

_____

_____

_____

_____

Email/Phone

Guest Name

_____

Wishes & Messages

_____

_____

_____

_____

_____

_____

_____

Email/Phone

Guest Name

_____

Wishes & Messages

_____

_____

_____

_____

_____

_____

_____

Email/Phone

Guest Name

_____

Wishes & Messages

_____

_____

_____

_____

_____

_____

Email/Phone

Guest Name

_____

Wishes & Messages

_____

_____

_____

_____

_____

_____

_____

Email/Phone

Guest Name

_____

Wishes & Messages

_____

_____

_____

_____

_____

_____

EMAIL/PHONE

Guest Name

_____

Wishes & Messages

_____

_____

_____

_____

_____

_____

_____

Email/Phone

Guest Name

_____

Wishes & Messages

_____

_____

_____

_____

_____

_____

_____

Email/Phone

Guest Name

_____

Wishes & Messages

_____

_____

_____

_____

_____

_____

_____

Email/Phone

Guest Name

Wishes & Messages

EMAIL/PHONE

Guest Name

_____

Wishes & Messages

_____

_____

_____

_____

_____

_____

✉ E

EMAIL/PHONE

Guest Name

_____

Wishes & Messages

_____

_____

_____

_____

_____

_____

Email/Phone

Guest Name

_____

Wishes & Messages

_____

_____

_____

_____

_____

_____

Email/Phone

Guest Name

_____

Wishes & Messages

_____

_____

_____

_____

_____

_____

EMAIL/PHONE

Guest Name

_____

Wishes & Messages

_____

_____

_____

_____

_____

_____

_____

Email/Phone

Guest Name

_____

Wishes & Messages

_____

_____

_____

_____

_____

_____

_____

Email/Phone

Guest Name

_____

Wishes & Messages

_____

_____

_____

_____

_____

_____

_____

Email/Phone

Guest Name

_____

Wishes & Messages

_____

_____

_____

_____

_____

_____

_____

Email/Phone

Guest Name

Wishes & Messages

Email/Phone

Guest Name

_____

Wishes & Messages

_____

_____

_____

_____

_____

_____

Email/Phone

Guest Name

_____

Wishes & Messages

_____

_____

_____

_____

_____

_____

_____

Email/Phone

Guest Name

_____

Wishes & Messages

_____

_____

_____

_____

_____

_____

Email/Phone

Guest Name

Wishes & Messages

_____

_____

_____

_____

_____

_____

_____

Email/Phone

Guest Name

_____

Wishes & Messages

_____

_____

_____

_____

_____

_____

Email/Phone

Guest Name

Wishes & Messages

✉ Email/Phone

Guest Name

_____

Wishes & Messages

_____

_____

_____

_____

_____

_____

Email/Phone

Guest Name

_____

Wishes & Messages

_____

_____

_____

_____

_____

_____

_____

Email/Phone

Guest Name

_____

Wishes & Messages

_____

_____

_____

_____

_____

_____

EMAIL/PHONE

Guest Name

_____

Wishes & Messages

_____

_____

_____

_____

_____

_____

_____

✉ Email/Phone

Guest Name

_____

Wishes & Messages

_____

_____

_____

_____

_____

_____

EMAIL/PHONE

Guest Name

_____

Wishes & Messages

_____

_____

_____

_____

_____

_____

_____

✉ Email/Phone

Guest Name

_____

Wishes & Messages

_____

_____

_____

_____

_____

_____

_____

EMAIL/PHONE

Guest Name

Wishes & Messages

✉ E
Email/Phone

Guest Name

_____

Wishes & Messages

_____

_____

_____

_____

_____

_____

Email/Phone

Guest Name

Wishes & Messages

✉ **Email/Phone**

Guest Name

_____

Wishes & Messages

_____

_____

_____

_____

_____

_____

EMAIL/PHONE

Guest Name

_____

Wishes & Messages

_____

_____

_____

_____

_____

_____

_____

✉ **Email/Phone**

Guest Name

_____

Wishes & Messages

_____

_____

_____

_____

_____

_____

Email/Phone

Guest Name

_____

Wishes & Messages

_____
_____
_____
_____
_____
_____
_____

Email/Phone

Guest Name

_____

Wishes & Messages

_____

_____

_____

_____

_____

_____

_____

EMAIL/PHONE

Guest Name

Wishes & Messages

✉ Email/Phone

Guest Name

_____

Wishes & Messages

_____

_____

_____

_____

_____

_____

_____

EMAIL/PHONE

Guest Name

_____

Wishes & Messages

_____

_____

_____

_____

_____

_____

Email/Phone

Guest Name

Wishes & Messages

✉ **Email/Phone**

Guest Name

_____

Wishes & Messages

_____

_____

_____

_____

_____

_____

_____

Email/Phone

Guest Name

_____

Wishes & Messages

_____

_____

_____

_____

_____

_____

Email/Phone

Guest Name

_____

Wishes & Messages

_____

_____

_____

_____

_____

_____

_____

Email/Phone

Guest Name

_____

Wishes & Messages

_____

_____

_____

_____

_____

_____

_____

Email/Phone

Guest Name

_____

Wishes & Messages

_____

_____

_____

_____

_____

_____

_____

Email/Phone

Guest Name

_____

Wishes & Messages

_____

_____

_____

_____

_____

_____

_____

Email/Phone

Guest Name

Wishes & Messages

Email/Phone

Guest Name

_____

Wishes & Messages

_____

_____

_____

_____

_____

_____

EMAIL/PHONE

Guest Name

_____

Wishes & Messages

_____

_____

_____

_____

_____

_____

_____

Email/Phone

Guest Name

_____

Wishes & Messages

_____

_____

_____

_____

_____

_____

EMAIL/PHONE

Guest Name

Wishes & Messages

Email/Phone

Guest Name

Wishes & Messages

Email/Phone

Guest Name

_____

Wishes & Messages

_____

_____

_____

_____

_____

_____

_____

✉ EMAIL/PHONE

Guest Name

_____

Wishes & Messages

_____

_____

_____

_____

_____

_____

Email/Phone

Guest Name

Wishes & Messages

✉ E

EMAIL/PHONE

Guest Name

_____

Wishes & Messages

_____

_____

_____

_____

_____

_____

Email/Phone

Guest Name

_____

Wishes & Messages

_____

_____

_____

_____

_____

_____

_____

EMAIL/PHONE

Guest Name

_____

Wishes & Messages

_____

_____

_____

_____

_____

_____

EMAIL/PHONE

Guest Name

_____

Wishes & Messages

_____

_____

_____

_____

_____

_____

_____

Email/Phone

Guest Name

_____

Wishes & Messages

_____

_____

_____

_____

_____

_____

_____

Email/Phone

Guest Name

_____

Wishes & Messages

_____
_____
_____
_____
_____
_____
_____

Email/Phone

Guest Name

_____

Wishes & Messages

_____

_____

_____

_____

_____

_____

Email/Phone

Guest Name

Wishes & Messages

_____

_____

_____

_____

_____

_____

_____

Email/Phone

Guest Name

_____

Wishes & Messages

_____

_____

_____

_____

_____

_____

_____

Email/Phone

Guest Name

Wishes & Messages

✉ E

EMAIL/PHONE

Guest Name

Wishes & Messages

EMAIL/PHONE

Guest Name

_____

Wishes & Messages

_____

_____

_____

_____

_____

_____

Email/Phone

Guest Name

_____

Wishes & Messages

_____

_____

_____

_____

_____

_____

Email/Phone

Guest Name

_____

Wishes & Messages

_____

_____

_____

_____

_____

_____

_____

✉ Email/Phone

Guest Name

_____

Wishes & Messages

_____

_____

_____

_____

_____

_____

_____

Email/Phone

Guest Name

_____

Wishes & Messages

_____

_____

_____

_____

_____

_____

_____

Email/Phone

Guest Name

_____

Wishes & Messages

_____

_____

_____

_____

_____

_____

EMAIL/PHONE

Guest Name

_____

Wishes & Messages

_____

_____

_____

_____

_____

_____

Email/Phone

Guest Name

_____

Wishes & Messages

_____

_____

_____

_____

_____

_____

Email/Phone

Guest Name

_____

Wishes & Messages

_____

_____

_____

_____

_____

_____

Email/Phone

Guest Name

_____

Wishes & Messages

_____

_____

_____

_____

_____

_____

EMAIL/PHONE

Guest Name

_____

Wishes & Messages

_____

_____

_____

_____

_____

_____

_____

✉ Email/Phone

Guest Name

_____

Wishes & Messages

_____

_____

_____

_____

_____

_____

Email/Phone

Guest Name

_____

Wishes & Messages

_____

_____

_____

_____

_____

_____

_____

EMAIL/PHONE

Guest Name

_____

Wishes & Messages

_____

_____

_____

_____

_____

_____

EMAIL/PHONE

Guest Name

_____

Wishes & Messages

_____

_____

_____

_____

_____

_____

Email/Phone

Guest Name

_____

Wishes & Messages

_____

_____

_____

_____

_____

_____

EMAIL/PHONE

Guest Name

_____

Wishes & Messages

_____

_____

_____

_____

_____

_____

_____

✉ E
Email/Phone

Guest Name

_____

Wishes & Messages

_____

_____

_____

_____

_____

_____

_____

EMAIL/PHONE

Guest Name

_____

Wishes & Messages

_____

_____

_____

_____

_____

_____

Email/Phone

Guest Name

_____

Wishes & Messages

_____

_____

_____

_____

_____

_____

_____

EMAIL/PHONE

Guest Name

Wishes & Messages

Email/Phone

Guest Name

_____

Wishes & Messages

_____

_____

_____

_____

_____

_____

Email/Phone

Guest Name

_____

Wishes & Messages

_____

_____

_____

_____

_____

_____

EMAIL/PHONE

Guest Name

_____

Wishes & Messages

_____

_____

_____

_____

_____

_____

_____

Email/Phone

Guest Name

Wishes & Messages

✉ E

Email/Phone

NOTES & PHOTOS

NOTES & PHOTOS

NOTES & PHOTOS

NOTES & PHOTOS

NOTES & PHOTOS

GIFT LOG

Name / Email / Phone	Gift

GIFT LOG

Name / Email / Phone	Gift

GIFT LOG

Name / Email / Phone	Gift

GIFT LOG

Name / Email / Phone	Gift

GIFT LOG

Name / Email / Phone	Gift

GIFT LOG

Name / Email / Phone	Gift

GIFT LOG

Name /Email /Phone	Gift

www.ingramcontent.com/pod-product-compliance
Lightning Source LLC
Chambersburg PA
CBHW080744240825
31568CB00038B/220